NEW CREATION
Confession Book

by Soonae Choi

Word of Faith Co.

New Creation Confession Book

Publishing Date _ May 22, 2024
Author _ Pastor Soonae Choi
ⓒ 2024 by Word of Faith Company
50 Guseong-ro, Giheung-gu, Yongin-si, Gyeonggi-do,
Republic of Korea, 16920
http://faithbook.kr
ISBN 979-11-981352-7-8 02230
Price : $10
Printed in Korea

contents

How to Effectively Utilize Confession _ 7

Part I **A New Creation's Prayer of Confession**
Apostle Paul's Prayer _ 14
I am a new creation _ 17
I know who I am in Christ _ 21
I know what I have as a Christian _ 38
I change situations and always win _ 58
I am the prophet of my life _ 63
Christ in me _ 66
Confession for Functioning in the Spirit _ 69

Part II **Prayer by Themes**
Confession for Healing _ 76
Confession for Financial Prosperity _ 80
Confession for a Victorious Family _ 86

Confession for Soul-winning _ 94
Confession for Peace _ 97
Confession for Wisdom and Guidance _ 100
Confession for Victory in Face of Trials _ 103
Confession for Overcoming Fear _ 107
Prayer for Beginning the Day _ 113

Part Ⅲ **Appendix**
Confessions from Foundation of Faith _ 120
Confessions from Psalms _ 138
Romans 8 _ 144
Isaiah 60 _ 150

Part Ⅳ **Understanding the Principles of Confession** _ 155

How to Effectively Utilize Confession

Hallelujah! Praise Jesus Christ, who achieved everything and gave us his authority and power so that we could reign in every situation and live a victorious life.

Living a life of faith, partnering with the Holy Spirit as a child of the Father, and serving Jesus Christ as Lord is truly an amazing life.

The moment we accept the gospel and are born again with this new life, our spirit has become a new man. However, because our mind, emotion, and will, which belong to the soul, have not been renewed, we must renew them through God's Word and continually train our born again spirit by functioning in faith according to the Word. Only then can we gradually develop spiritually and fully reign in this new life as a king.

Praying in tongues, meditating on the word (confession), the attitude of putting God's Word as your highest priority, and training to immediately obey the voice of our born again spirit is the shortcut that allow us to develop our born again spirit and reign in every situation.

As I have been in ministry for decades, I see that even though people might know much scripture, if they do not confess with their mouth the Word they believe, they experience very slow positive changes and weak mani-festations. On the other hand, I have also seen that no matter how bad the mental problem, if a person receives God's Word as truth and repeatedly confesses it, he or she can be completely restored from a hopeless situation, built up to be an ambassador for God's kingdom.

Confessing the Word is not just a method you see on the outside. This is the spiritual principle of how Jesus manifested in the natural realm what he already achieved in the spiritual realm, and is a power and privilege that only new creation born-again Christians can have.

Now I have a few necessary words to share with you about how to utilize "The New Creation Confession Book" more effectively.

- Confess with a strong and bold heart. If you are saying that 'There is nothing I can do about this situation or circumstance. I have no hope but God's compassion,' this kind of attitude is from the Old Testament, and is not the attitude that allows you to reign as a king as a joint-heir with Christ. Remember that before God told Joshua "Let not the Word to depart from your mouth that you may keep and do all that is written therein," God first told him to "Be strong and courageous." Have strength from the heart just as David had when he went out to fight Goliath.

- Be conscious of what the Bible says about who you are in Christ, what you have in Christ, and what you can do in Christ as you confess as a born-again new creation.

- When you confess, it is good to not just say it with your mouth, but to put your heart and emotion into it, confessing as loud as you can.

- If there is a Scripture that touches your heart or if you think it to be important to you at this moment, confess those Scriptures repeatedly several times with gusto, praying in tongues intermittently, having the anointing overflow from your spirit.

- If you want to build a bold attitude before you confess, confess "I Change Situations and Always Win," "I Am the Prophet of My Life," and "Christ In Me" first.

- Always confess "The New Creation Confession" first, and then confess from "Confession by Themes," picking a prayer theme that applies to the problem you are facing now.

- It is always good to praise and worship God, to thank him, and to pray in tongues in between your confession. Every confession seeks the manifestations of the Holy Spirit who works according to the Word of God.

When we confess the Word with faith, we first receive revelation in our hearts, coming to understand and believe the Word. When this happens, you will find that even if we do not put great effort, the Word we confessed becomes the power within us, producing whatever it has talked about. Then the situation will change, or the wisdom to change the situation will follow. This is because the more we look at the Word, the more the glory of the Word is at work in us.

But we all, with unveiled face, beholding as in a mirror the glory of the Lord, are being transformed into the same image from glory to glory, just as by the Spirit of the Lord.   2 Corinthians 3:18

God has already prepared all good things in the spiritual realm and he has given us the authority and responsibility to execute them here on this earth.

We must each reign in all situations regarding each of our lives, gradually increasing in influence, winning souls, and expanding God's kingdom as soldiers for God's kingdom. Hallelujah!

Looking forward to the march of a great army fulfilling God's will here on this earth⋯

June 1st, 2011
Soonae Choi

Metamorphosis

Part I

A New Creation's Prayer of Confession

> That the sharing of your faith
> may become effective by the acknowledgment
> of every good thing which is in you in Christ Jesus.
> **Philemon 1:6**

Apostle Paul's Prayer

Prayer for Revelation

That the God of our Lord Jesus Christ, the Father of glory, may give to you the spirit of wisdom and revelation in the knowledge of Him, the eyes of your understanding being enlightened; that you may know what is the hope of His calling, what are the riches of the glory of His inheritance in the saints, and what is the exceeding greatness of His power toward us who believe, according to the working of His mighty power.

Ephesians 1:17-19

Prayer for Power

That He would grant you, according to the riches of His glory, to be strengthened with might through His Spirit in the inner man, that Christ may dwell in your hearts through faith; that you, being rooted and grounded in love, may be able to comprehend with all the saints what is the width and length and depth and height -- to know the love of Christ which passes knowledge; that you may be filled with all the fullness of God.

Ephesians 3:16-19

Prayer for Fruitfulness

For this reason we also, since the day we heard it, do not cease to pray for you, and to ask that you may be filled with the knowledge of His will in all wisdom and spiritual understanding; that you may walk worthy of the Lord, fully pleasing Him, being fruitful in every good work and increasing in the knowledge of God; strengthened with all might, according to His glorious power, for all patience and longsuffering with joy; giving thanks to the Father who has qualified us to be partakers of the inheritance of the saints in the light.

Colossians 1:9-12

Prayer for Gospel Entrepreneurs

And this I pray, that your love may abound still more and more in knowledge and all discernment, that you may approve the things that are excellent, that you may be sincere and without offense till the day of Christ, being filled with the fruits of righteousness which are by Jesus Christ, to the glory and praise of God. Philippians 1:9-11

I am a new creation

Therefore, if anyone is in Christ, he is a new creation; old things have passed away; behold, all things have become new.   2 Corinthians 5:17

Having been born again, not of corruptible seed but incorruptible, through the word of God which lives and abides forever.   1 Peter 1:23

Of His own will He brought us forth by the word of truth, that we might be a kind of firstfruits of His creatures.   James 1:18

I have been crucified with Christ; it is no longer I who live, but Christ lives in me; and the life which I now live in the flesh I live by faith in the

Son of God, who loved me and gave Himself for me.   Galatians 2:20

For you are all sons of God through faith in Christ Jesus. For as many of you as were baptized into Christ have put on Christ.   Galatians 3:26-27

He has delivered us from the power of darkness and conveyed us into the kingdom of the Son of His love.   Colossians 1:13

For if by the one man's offense death reigned through the one, much more those who receive abundance of grace and of the gift of righteousness will reign in life through the One, Jesus Christ.   Romans 5:17

Therefore we do not lose heart. Even though our outward man is perishing, yet the inward man is being renewed day by day.   2 Corinthians 4:16

I was born again from heaven by receiving Jesus into my heart. He has delivered me from the power of darkness, and has translated me into the kingdom of his dear Son. I was crucified with Christ, but now I am quickened together with Christ and I sit together in heavenly places in Christ Jesus. His authority is my authority.

It is no longer I who live, but Christ lives in me. I have put on Christ. I have become a new creation; not partially changed but completely renewed in the realm of the spirit. I function in the realm of the spirit and in the realm of the Word as a new creation.

I have the nature of Christ. I have the love of Christ. I have the power of Christ. I can change things through my new nature when I think, speak and act according to the Word.

Now I am never disappointed by things or circumstances in the world, but I walk according to the Word of God to reign in life by Jesus Christ. I am never discouraged. For though my outward man perish, the inward man is renewed day by day, and I change from glory to glory and go from power above power.

I am a new creation born again with his divine life and nature.

I know who I am in Christ

They are not of the world, just as I am not of the world. Sanctify them by Your truth. Your word is truth. As You sent Me into the world, I also have sent them into the world.   John 17:16-18

But you have come to Mount Zion and to the city of the living God, the heavenly Jerusalem, to an innumerable company of angels, to the general assembly and church of the firstborn who are registered in heaven, to God the Judge of all, to the spirits of just men made perfect, to Jesus the Mediator of the new covenant, and to the blood of sprinkling that speaks better things than that of Abel.   Hebrews 12:22-24

Yet in all these things we are more than conquerors through Him who loved us. Romans 8:37

But you are a chosen generation, a royal priesthood, a holy nation, His own special people, that you may proclaim the praises of Him who called you out of darkness into His marvelous light;
1 Peter 2:9

I know who I am in Christ.
I am a child of God.
I live in the world but I am not of the world.
I am a citizen of Zion.
Therefore, I live according to the spiritual principles of Zion. John 17:16, Hebrews 12:22
I am from above.
I live a supernatural life by faith.
Nothing can make me a victim.
I am more than a conqueror who has overcome the world and I reign in this world supernaturally. Romans 8:37

Thank you, Jesus. I know who I am.

I am a new creation in Christ. 2 Corinthians 5:17

I live by the life of God, the same life Jesus had. 1 John 4:17

You have given me all things that pertain unto life and godliness, through the cross by your divine power. 2 Peter 1:3

Wherever my feet tread upon, those promises in your Word are already guaranteed. Joshua 1:3

1. I have eternal life

For God so loved the world that He gave His only begotten Son, that whoever believes in Him should not perish but have everlasting life.

John 3:16

In Him was life, and the life was the light of men.

John 1:4

But these are written that you may believe that Jesus is the Christ, the Son of God, and that believing you may have life in His name.

John 20:31

And this is the testimony : that God has given us eternal life, and this life is in His Son. He who has the Son has life; he who does not have the Son of God does not have life.   1 John 5:11-12

I have eternal life. This eternal life is the God-kind of life (ZOE), and it has been given to me when I received Jesus.

My spirit is full of ZOE. My soul is full of ZOE. My body is full of ZOE.

ZOE is a life-giving spirit. Therefore, no sickness can stay in my body. Any infirmity or disease cannot stand but leave.

When I am confronted with circumstances I do not like, I declare by faith to change the situation. When I declare in ZOE, situations cannot help but change.

2. I have conquered the devil

Inasmuch then as the children have partaken of flesh and blood, He Himself likewise shared in the same, that through death He might destroy him who had the power of death, that is, the devil, and release those who through fear of death were all their lifetime subject to bondage.

Hebrews 2:14-15

Having wiped out the handwriting of requirements that was against us, which was contrary to us. And He has taken it out of the way, having nailed it to the cross. Having disarmed principalities and powers, He made a public spectacle of them, triumphing over them in it. Colossians 2:14-15

You are of God, little children, and have overcome them, because He who is in you is greater than he who is in the world. 1 John 4:4

And they overcame him by the blood of the Lamb and by the word of their testimony, and they did not love their lives to the death.   Revelation 12:11

Being in Christ, I have overcome the devil. I do not fear the devil. The devil has nothing to do with me. Therefore, I always win. This is because greater is he that is in me than he that is in the world.

3. I have faith

For I say, through the grace given to me, to everyone who is among you, not to think of himself more highly than he ought to think, but to think soberly, as God has dealt to each one a measure of faith.

Romans 12:3

For we walk by faith, not by sight.

2 Corinthians 5:7

I have faith. It has been given to me when I was born again and it has the power to move mountains.

I do not walk by sight. I walk by faith. Because I think, speak, and act in the realm of faith, I always win. I increase my faith by hearing the Word, and as I act on my faith, my faith gets stronger. I overcome the world by faith.

4. I became righteous by the righteousness of God

But of Him you are in Christ Jesus, who became for us wisdom from God - and righteousness and sanctification and redemption - 1 Corinthians 1:30

Being justified freely by His grace through the redemption that is in Christ Jesus,   Romans 3:24

Who was delivered up because of our offenses, and was raised because of our justification. Therefore, having been justified by faith, we have peace with God through our Lord Jesus Christ,
Romans 4:25-5:1

For He made Him who knew no sin to be sin for us, that we might become the righteousness of God in Him.   2 Corinthians 5:21

I am righteous. Because Christ became my righteousness, I became righteous. I was born again righteous by the new birth in faith. Righteousness is my nature.

No matter what I do, I can always stand before the presence of God without any condemnation or a sense of inferiority.

My spirit always has the ability to do the will of God. I am always bold. As a righteous man, my prayers always work. Therefore, I always get my prayers answered.

5. I have grace which enables me to do all things with excellence

But to each one of us grace was given according to the measure of Christ's gift.   Ephesians 4:7

I can do all things through Christ who strengthens me.   Philippians 4:13

And we know that all things work together for good to those who love God, to those who are the called according to His purpose.
     Romans 8:28

But the anointing which you have received from Him abides in you, and you do not need that anyone teach you; but as the same anointing teaches you concerning all things, and is true, and is not a lie, and just as it has taught you, you will abide in Him.   1John 2:27

He was well known for his intellectual brilliance and spiritual wisdom ⋯ He could do anything- interpret dreams, solve mysteries, explain puzzles.   Daniel 5:12(MSG)

I have grace flowing out of my spirit, so my life is full of your beauty, favor, charm and dignity.

Because of this grace, I am always favored by people. I am favored by my superiors, colleagues, friends, and subordinates.

This grace is God's ability to overcome any situation against me. God's ability is working in my spirit.

I can do all things through Christ who gives me the ability. God is my ability. I am not using human abilities. I have supernatural ability. I can do all things.

My mind is anointed. My spirit is anointed.

I am excellent. Joseph received an excellent spirit. Daniel also received an excellent spirit. I have also received an excellent spirit. Nothing is impossible unto me. God's ability is working in me.

No weapon formed against me shall prosper, because greater is he that is in me, than he that is in the world. God is my ability.

6. I am a legal and actual son of God with God's life

Behold what manner of love the Father has bestowed on us, that we should be called children of God! Therefore the world does not know us, because it did not know Him. Beloved, now we are children of God; and it has not yet been revealed what we shall be, but we know that when He is revealed, we shall be like Him, for we shall see Him as He is.   1 John 3:1-2

And because you are sons, God has sent forth the Spirit of His Son into your hearts, crying out, "Abba, Father!"   Galatian 4:6

Jesus said to her, "Do not cling to Me, for I have not yet ascended to My Father; but go to My brethren and say to them, 'I am ascending to My Father and your Father, and to My God and your God.'"   John 20:17

Because I am a son of God, I can call him, Abba, Father.

God sent his only begotten son to the world so that we could dwell in him.

I reign in this world as Jesus reigned in this world.

I refuse to be sick.

I refuse to fail.

I am more than a conqueror through him that loved me.

I am blessed.

Blessings follow me wherever I go.

Because Jesus brought eternal life, I live the same class of life as him.

I am an ark of blessing. I live like a king in the world. As a king speaks with authority, I speak like a king. My words come to pass.

I'm not ordinary.

7. I am the righteousness of God

For He made Him who knew no sin to be sin for us, that we might become the righteousness of God in Him.   2 Corinthians 5:21

The work of righteousness will be peace, And the effect of righteousness, quietness and assurance forever.   Isaiah 32:17

But you are a chosen race, a royal priesthood, a dedicated nation, [God's] own [a]purchased, special people, that you may set forth the wonderful deeds and display the virtues and perfections of Him Who called you out of darkness into His marvelous light.
    1 Peter 2:9(AMPC)

    I am the righteousness of God. I am the trophy of his goodness. I am his ambassador. I am his messenger.

People come to know God through me. People see that God is alive and working through me.

Every part of my life represents the glory of God.

I know what I have as a Christian

1. I have the God-kind of life

The thief does not come except to steal, and to kill, and to destroy. I have come that they may have life, and that they may have it more abundantly.

John 10:10

That whoever believes in Him should not perish but have eternal life. For God so loved the world that He gave His only begotten Son, that whoever believes in Him should not perish but have everlasting life.
John 3:15-16

He who believes in the Son has everlasting life; and he who does not believe the Son shall not see life, but the wrath of God abides on him.

John 3:36

I have eternal life. Eternal life is the life of God, and this life was given to me when I received Jesus into my heart.

My spirit is full of ZOE. My soul is full of ZOE. My body is full of ZOE. This ZOE life is a life-giving spirit. Therefore, no sickness can dwell in my body. All weaknesses and diseases cannot stay in my body.

If I meet a circumstance I do not like, I proclaim by faith to change the situation. When I proclaim in this ZOE life by faith, the situation cannot help but change.

2. I have righteousness

Being justified freely by His grace through the redemption that is in Christ Jesus,   Romans 3:24

Who was delivered up because of our offenses, and was raised because of our justification.
Romans 4:25

For He made Him who knew no sin to be sin for us, that we might become the righteousness of God in Him.   2 Corinthians 5:21

But of Him you are in Christ Jesus, who became for us wisdom from God - and righteousness and sanctification and redemption -   1 Corinthians 1:30

And be found in Him, not having my own righteousness, which is from the law, but that which is through faith in Christ, the righteousness which is from God by faith;   Philippians 3:9

I am righteous. Christ has become my righteousness, and therefore, I am righteous.

Righteousness is my nature. I can always stand in the presence of God without any sense of guilt or inferiority regardless of my actions.

My spirit has the ability to always act according to God's will.

I am always righteous. Therefore, my prayers are always answered.

3. I have the remission of sins

For this is My blood of the new covenant, which is shed for many for the remission of sins.
Matthew 26:28

For if our heart condemns us, God is greater than our heart, and knows all things.   1 John 3:20

How much more shall the blood of Christ, who through the eternal Spirit offered Himself without spot to God, cleanse your conscience from dead works to serve the living God?   Hebrews 9:14

To Him all the prophets witness that, through His name, whoever believes in Him will receive remission of sins.   Acts 10:43

   My sins have been remitted. I am a righteous man and I am no longer a sinner. If I sin, I confess my sins and quickly step out of condemnation.
   My sins have been completely remitted.

4. I have salvation, deliverance, and freedom

He has delivered us from the power of darkness and conveyed us into the kingdom of the Son of His love, Colossians 1:13

The Spirit of the LORD is upon Me, Because He has anointed Me To preach the gospel to the poor; He has sent Me to heal the brokenhearted, To proclaim liberty to the captives And recovery of sight to the blind, To set at liberty those who are oppressed; To proclaim the acceptable year of the LORD. Luke 4:18-19

To open their eyes, in order to turn them from darkness to light, and from the power of Satan to God, that they may receive forgiveness of sins and an inheritance among those who are sanctified by faith in Me. Acts 26:18

I know who I am. I am a child of God. I am a joint-heir with Christ.

Everything in this world must obey to the name of Jesus.

I have overcome Satan. Christ has brought me out from the kingdom of darkness and has freed me into the kingdom of his dear Son.

Now the devil has nothing to do with me. Satan cannot manifest in any area of my life.

I declare Satan's manifestations to be illegal in any area of my life.

"Satan, I command you in the name of Jesus, leave me!"

5. I have healing and divine health

But He was wounded for our transgressions, He was bruised for our iniquities; The chastisement for our peace was upon Him, And by His stripes we are healed. Isaiah 53:5

Who Himself bore our sins in His own body on the tree, that we, having died to sins, might live for righteousness--by whose stripes you were healed. 1 Peter 2:24

Healing and divine health are mine.

By Christ's stripes I am healed. Therefore, I refuse every weakness and sickness in Jesus name. No sickness can stay in my body.

Divine health is our birthright. I am always full of God's power and God's life.

I am going to live a long and healthy life, glorifying God with the divine health God has given me.

6. I have peace and oneness with God

For He Himself is our peace, who has made both one, and has broken down the middle wall of separation, having abolished in His flesh the enmity, that is, the law of commandments contained in ordinances, so as to create in Himself one new man from the two, thus making peace,

Ephesians 2:14-15

Therefore, having been justified by faith, we have peace with God through our Lord Jesus Christ, through whom also we have access by faith into this grace in which we stand, and rejoice in hope of the glory of God.   Romans 5:1-2

These things I have spoken to you, that in Me you may have peace. In the world you will have tribulation; but be of good cheer, I have overcome the world.   John 16:33

Through our Lord Christ Jesus, I have peace with God.

I have become one with God through Christ. Jesus is the head and we are his body.

We are members of his flesh and of his bones.

Ephesians 5:30

As Jesus was on this earth, so am I.

7. I have prosperity

For you know the grace of our Lord Jesus Christ, that though He was rich, yet for your sakes He became poor, that you through His poverty might become rich.   2 Corinthians 8:9

And God is able to make all grace abound toward you, that you, always having all sufficiency in all things, may have an abundance for every good work.   2 Corinthians 9:8

Now may He who supplies seed to the sower, and bread for food, supply and multiply the seed you have sown and increase the fruits of your righteousness,   2 Corinthians 9:10

The LORD was with Joseph, and he was a successful man; and he was in the house of his master the Egyptian.   Genesis 39:2

Believe in the LORD your God, and you shall be established; believe His prophets, and you shall prosper. 2 Chronicles 20:20

Let them shout for joy and be glad, Who favor my righteous cause; And let them say continually, "Let the LORD be magnified, Who has pleasure in the prosperity of His servant." Psalm 35:27

The blessing of the LORD makes one rich, And He adds no sorrow with it. Proverbs 10:22

Again proclaim, saying, Thus says the LORD of hosts : My cities shall again spread out through prosperity; Zechariah 1:17

Jesus Christ who was rich became poor so that I may become rich. Therefore, being born again, I am rich.

Prosperity is an authority that belongs to a child of God. Prosperity is God's gift. God gives me the ability, wisdom, and opportunity to obtain wealth.

I have an excellent spirit that best utilizes the wisdom, ability, opportunity, and divine connection God gives me.

As God's soldier, I use the prosperity God has given me to win souls and to expand God's kingdom.

I am prosperous.

8. As a citizen of Zion, I have the authority to use the name of Jesus

And Jesus came and spoke to them, saying, All authority has been given to Me in heaven and on earth. Go therefore and make disciples of all the nations, baptizing them in the name of the Father and of the Son and of the Holy Spirit, teaching them to observe all things that I have commanded you; and lo, I am with you always, even to the end of the age. Amen.   Matthew 28:18-20

And if children, then heirs--heirs of God and joint heirs with Christ, if indeed we suffer with Him, that we may also be glorified together.

Romans 8:17

For we are God's [own] handiwork (His workmanship), recreated in Christ Jesus, [born anew] that we may do those good works which God predestined (planned beforehand) for us [taking paths which He prepared ahead of time], that we should walk in them [living the good life which He prearranged and made ready for us to live.

Ephesians 2:10(AMPC)

You did not choose Me, but I chose you and appointed you that you should go and bear fruit, and that your fruit should remain, that whatever you ask the Father in My name He may give you.

John 15:16

Jesus took back the authority to rule this earth and made me a joint-heir with him to give me that authority.

Whatever I see according to the Word, whatever I believe, and whatever I proclaim in Jesus name, everything obeys the authority of that name. I am a conqueror reigning in my life with Christ.

9. I have God's agape love poured inside me and I can walk in that love

And we have known and believed the love that God has for us. God is love, and he who abides in love abides in God, and God in him. Love has been perfected among us in this : that we may have boldness in the day of judgment; because as He is, so are we in this world. There is no fear in love; but perfect love casts out fear, because fear involves torment. But he who fears has not been made perfect in love. We love Him because He first loved us.   1 John 4:16-19

Now hope does not disappoint, because the love of God has been poured out in our hearts by the Holy Spirit who was given to us.   Romans 5:5

But I say to you, love your enemies, bless those who curse you, do good to those who hate you, and pray for those who spitefully use you and persecute you, Matthew 5:44

Love suffers long and is kind; love does not envy; love does not parade itself, is not puffed up; does not behave rudely, does not seek its own, is not provoked, thinks no evil; does not rejoice in iniquity, but rejoices in the truth; bears all things, believes all things, hopes all things, endures all things. 1 Corinthians 13:4-7

I always walk in love with the Holy Spirit inside me who is the spirit of love.

I love my enemies and bless those who curse me. I am kind to those who hate me and by praying for those who mistreat and persecute me, I act according to my heavenly Father's perfection.

I do not overcome darkness with darkness. Instead, I drive out darkness with light, because I am a child of my Father who is the light. I have that kind of love poured inside me. Therefore, I choose to love with the love of God.

I am patient.

I am meek.

I am not jealous.

I do not brag and I am not proud.

I am not rude.

I do not seek my own profit.

I do not get angry.

I do not think evil.

I do not rejoice in evil. I rejoice with the truth.

Because I am a lover, I cover all things with love, I believe all things, I desire all things, and I endure all things.

10. I have wisdom

But of Him you are in Christ Jesus, who became for us wisdom from God - and righteousness and sanctification and redemption -
1 Corinthians 1:30

In whom are hidden all the treasures of wisdom and knowledge ··· For in Him dwells all the fullness of the Godhead bodily; and you are complete in Him, who is the head of all principality and power.
Colossians 2:3, 9-10

The Spirit of the LORD shall rest upon Him, The Spirit of wisdom and understanding, The Spirit of counsel and might, The Spirit of knowledge and of the fear of the LORD.   Isaiah 11:2

Wisdom is the principal thing; Therefore get wisdom. And in all your getting, get understanding. Exalt her, and she will promote you; She will bring you honor, when you embrace her. Proverbs 4:7-8

Hear instruction and be wise, And do not disdain it. Blessed is the man who listens to me, Watching daily at my gates, Waiting at the posts of my doors. For whoever finds me finds life, And obtains favor from the LORD; Proverbs 8:33-35

Because Jesus became my wisdom, greater wisdom than Solomon's is inside me. Therefore, I always think the right thoughts, say the right things, and make the right choices and actions by the help of the Holy Spirit.

I am not misled. I do not walk in darkness. I always see with the right perspective and make wise choices and wise actions.

I change situations and always win

For assuredly, I say to you, whoever says to this mountain, 'Be removed and be cast into the sea,' and does not doubt in his heart, but believes that those things he says will be done, he will have whatever he says.   Mark 11:23

You are of God, little children, and have overcome them, because He who is in you is greater than he who is in the world.   1 John 4:4

For if by the one man's offense death reigned through the one, much more those who receive abundance of grace and of the gift of righteousness will reign in life through the One, Jesus Christ.)
                                                                 Romans 5:17

And they overcame him by the blood of the Lamb and by the word of their testimony, and they did not love their lives to the death.

> Revelations 12:11

I know who I am.

I am a victor in Christ.

I have changed my old way of thinking.

I have changed my thoughts and my heart.

I am a success.

Father, thank you for leading me today.

I worship the king of glory.

I go out with the Lord today.

I go with the Holy Spirit.

I know in my spirit the right direction I should go. I am going to see the right thing, and I will do the right thing.

Christ, the hope of glory, lives in me.

Wherever I go, there is favor to my left and to my right.

I have a reigning spirit. Therefore, I cannot fail.

I am not shaken by my surrounding circumstances or the people around me, because I am filled with the life of God and full of the Holy Spirit.

Father, I thank you in the name of Jesus. Hallelujah!

I am a child of God.

I have a new language.

This language is a language of the spirit.

This language is a victorious language.

I always win.

I know who I am.

I am always victorious.

Everyday, I improve and make progress.

I am moving forward.

I am a victor.

I got the Word of God in me.

I got the life of God in me.

Christ, the hope of glory, lives in me.

Christ fills my spirit.

Christ fills my soul.

Christ fills my body.

I carry his divine presence.

I am the light of the world.

I am walking in God's marvelous light.

There is no darkness there.

I function in God's glory.

I function in God's realm.

I function in God's realm of glory, which is the realm of victory.

I function in God's purpose.

I was born for the glory of God.

My life is full of God's glory.

I came to this world at the right time.

As God's Word enters my spirit, it enlightens me and gives me information, strengthens me, shows me the right direction to take, and builds me up.

This is all because I was born for the glory of God.

I bring God's blessing wherever I go.

I always give blessings wherever I go.

I am a citizen of Zion, God's kingdom.

I know who I am.

I bring change to any situation.

Therefore, I do not blame my circumstances.

I do not blame people, because I have the power to change situations.

I know who I am.

I am filled with the life of God.

I change situations by the power of God's Word and the Holy Spirit. Therefore, I always win.

Father, I thank you in the name of Jesus. Hallelujah!

I am the prophet of my life

God is not the only one determining how blessed or how cursed I would be. God has given me the power to choose my own destiny.

I change the course of my life with my mouth.

This Book of the Law shall not depart from your mouth, but you shall meditate in it day and night, that you may observe to do according to all that is written in it. For then you will make your way prosperous, and then you will have good success.

Joshua 1:8

I am getting healthier everyday.
I succeed more and more everyday.
I am getting stronger everyday.

I am growing in knowledge, understanding, and wisdom everyday.

God's ability is at work in me, and therefore, I cannot fail.

I am a success.

God's hand is upon my life, and I move forward and make progress.

God's ability is inside me.

The ability of the spirit is at work in me.

I see my future with anticipation because I have a great future ahead of me.

I see that all things are changing for the best.

I surely believe that everything God has spoken about me in his Word will come true. Therefore, I glorify God by being unshakable in the Word and strengthened in faith.

My health is improving.

My finances are increasing.

I am making progress.

I see prosperity.

I see my promotion.

Greater is he that is in me than he that is in the world.

I have the power of God working in me.

I can do all things through Christ who strengthens me.

The anointing of the Holy Spirit upon me helps me to advance forward.

I am getting better, stronger, and bigger everyday.

I walk in victory in the name of Jesus Christ.

Glory to God.

Christ in me

I can do all things through Christ who strengthens me. Philippians 4:13

I have been crucified with Christ. Yet, I still live. Now, it is no longer I that live but Christ living in me. The life I now live in the flesh, I live by faith in the son of God who loved me and gave himself for me. Galatians 2:20

My inner man is made strong by the spirit of the Father and his power. Christ dwells in my heart through faith. I am firmly rooted and grounded in love. I desire to know and possess the width and length, the height and depth of Christ's love. I know how much Christ loves me beyond mere head knowledge. I am filled with the fullness of God. My body is filled and overflowing with God.

His presence is always with me in utmost abundance. Ephesians 3:16-19

There is no darkness in my body and it is full of light. God is light. My body is full of the nature and power of God. Luke 11:36, 1 John 1:5

Because Christ lives in my body, I am filled with the fullness of the Godhead bodily. Colossians 2:9-10

Christ lives in me. Christ is my hope of glory. Christ is the glory that I can see and anticipate. Colossians 1:27

I am God's son. I can call my heavenly Father, "Abba, Father," because he has given me the Spirit of his Son. Christ in me prays, "Abba, Father! All things are possible for you." Galatians 4:6, Mark 14:36

I have the same glory God the Father has given Jesus. That glory speaks that "I and the Father are one." I am one with God. John 10:30

Christ lives in me. I am one with Christ. I am one with the Father. John 10:30

My Father works through Christ living in me. Through this, the world knows that the Father has sent Christ to live in me. Through this, the world knows that the Father loves me the same way he loved Jesus. John 17:23

Christ, the Anointed One, lives in my body. The Father lives in me. I am one with the Father. John 10:30

Confession for Functioning in the Spirit

1. I believe in the power of the Word

So the word of the Lord grew mightily and prevailed. Acts 19:20

So now, brethren, I commend you to God and to the word of His grace, which is able to build you up and give you an inheritance among all those who are sanctified. Acts 20:32

It is the Spirit who gives life; the flesh profits nothing. The words that I speak to you are spirit, and they are life. John 6:63

I was born of the Word.

I receive the Word of God into my spirit with gladness.

When the Word enters my spirit I am edified.

When the Word of God prevails in my spirit, my ability increases and my life is changed.

The Word of God is able to build me up and give me an inheritance in Christ Jesus.

When I hear the Word and proclaim it, that Word works in my spirit and builds me up, and my ability is increased and my life is changed.

As I receive the word, I am being prepared for greater success.

Everything I ask for I receive. I win many souls and I bear much fruit.

2. I am conscious of what's inside me

And this is the testimony : that God has given us eternal life, and this life is in His Son. He who has the Son has life; he who does not have the Son of God does not have life. These things I have written to you who believe in the name of the Son of God, that you may know that you have eternal life, and that you may continue to believe in the name of the Son of God. 1 John 5:11-13

I can do all things through Christ who strengthens me. Philippians 4:13

However, when He, the Spirit of truth, has come, He will guide you into all truth; for He will not speak on His own authority, but whatever He hears He will speak; and He will tell you things to come. John 16:13

I am conscious of the life inside me.

I have eternal life. Eternal life is the life of God and this eternal life was given inside of me when I accepted Jesus.

My spirit is full of ZOE.

My soul is full of ZOE.

My body is full of ZOE.

This eternal life is a life-giving spirit. No sickness can stay in my body.

I live a supernatural life.

I have Christ consciousness.

I am one with Christ.

I no longer live by my own ability. I live by Christ's ability in me. I can do anything with this ability. My excellence is his ability.

I am conscious of the Holy Spirit. He lives in me.

The Holy Spirit teaches me, leads me into all truth, and instructs me. When I receive his instruction and change accordingly, I always win.

I am conscious of the Holy Spirit.

3. I'm a soul-winner

For God so loved the world that He gave His only begotten Son, that whoever believes in Him should not perish but have everlasting life.   John 3:16

For I am not ashamed of the gospel of Christ, for it is the power of God to salvation for everyone who believes, for the Jew first and also for the Greek.   Romans 1:16

The thief does not come except to steal, and to kill, and to destroy. I have come that they may have life, and that they may have it more abundantly.   John 10:10

And Jesus came and spoke to them, saying, All authority has been given to Me in heaven and on earth. Go therefore and make disciples of all the nations, baptizing them in the name of the Father and of the Son and of the Holy Spirit, teaching them to observe all things that I have commanded you; and lo, I am with you always, even to the end of the age. Amen. Matthew 28:18-20

I'm a soul-winner. God so loved the world that he sent his only begotten Son as a soul-winner.

Jesus loved souls that he gave his life to save those souls. I also love God and love souls, and therefore, I win souls. I'm a soul-winner.

Soul-winning is an act of love. Soul-winning is an act of faith. I am a soul-winner.

When I pray for a soul, I look at him with the eyes of the Lord and share the gospel. The price for that soul has already been paid and there is power to save in the gospel I preach. As long as he accepts the gospel, I know he can enter into a victorious and beautiful life. His life shall be like the rising son, shining brighter and brighter unto a perfect day.

I win souls anytime and anywhere. I'm a soul-winner. Soul-winning is my reason for life. It is my life's direction. I'm a soul-winner.

Metamorphosis

Part II

Prayer by Themes

For if by the one man's offense
death reigned through the one, much more those
who receive abundance of grace
and of the gift of righteousness will
reign in life through the One, Jesus Christ.
Romans 5:17

Confession for Healing

and said, "If you diligently heed the voice of the LORD your God and do what is right in His sight, give ear to His commandments and keep all His statutes, I will put none of the diseases on you which I have brought on the Egyptians. For I am the LORD who heals you." Exodus 15:26

Bless the LORD, O my soul; And all that is within me, bless His holy name! Bless the LORD, O my soul, And forget not all His benefits : Who forgives all your iniquities, Who heals all your diseases, Who redeems your life from destruction, Who crowns you with lovingkindness and tender mercies, Who satisfies your mouth with good things, So that your youth is renewed like the eagle's. Psalm 103:1-5

But He was wounded for our transgressions, He was bruised for our iniquities; The chastisement for our peace was upon Him, And by His stripes we are healed. Isaiah 53:5

How God anointed Jesus of Nazareth with the Holy Spirit and with power, who went about doing good and healing all who were oppressed by the devil, for God was with Him. Acts 10:38

That it might be fulfilled which was spoken by Isaiah the prophet, saying : "He Himself took our infirmities And bore our sicknesses."

Matthew 8:17

Who Himself bore our sins in His own body on the tree, that we, having died to sins, might live for righteousness--by whose stripes you were healed. 1 Peter 2:24

Lord, I believe in the Word of God that says Jesus Christ is the same yesterday, today, and forever. Jesus went everywhere teaching the Word and spreading the gospel of the kingdom of God and healed many people of diseases while living here on this earth.

Because I believe that Jesus is the same even today, I know he wants to heal me when I'm sick.

God's Word is my life and that Word brings healing to my body. I thank you that the Word has healing power. Father, I will not take my eyes off of your Word. I will plant your Word in the deepest part of my heart and guard it with all diligence.

I thank you that by Christ's stripes I am healed. I act in faith. I do not live by what I see. I refuse every symptom caused by sickness in Jesus name. Praise the name of the Lord. Jesus, I love you. Thank for healing me and protecting my health.

I refuse any sickness or pain in my body. Such

things can no longer stay in my body. I am full of God's life and power. By the divine health God gives me, I live a long and healthy life.

Just as the Lord has promised, Jesus has delivered me from all the curses of sickness. I cast out all the symptoms in my body with the Word of God. Eternal life flows in my body, in my spirit, and in my soul. Therefore, I declare that no sickness can exist in this eternal life.

The weak parts of my body are being restored. Jesus bore the stripes and by believing this truth I am healed.

Confession for Financial Prosperity

Let them shout for joy and be glad, Who favor my righteous cause; And let them say continually, "Let the LORD be magnified, Who has pleasure in the prosperity of His servant." Psalm 35:27

The blessing of the LORD makes one rich, And He adds no sorrow with it. Proverbs 10:22

Again proclaim, saying, Thus says the LORD of hosts : My cities shall again spread out through prosperity; Zechariah 1:17

For you know the grace of our Lord Jesus Christ, that though He was rich, yet for your sakes He became poor, that you through His poverty might become rich. 2 Corinthians 8:9

And God is able to make all grace abound toward you, that you, always having all sufficiency in all things, may have an abundance for every good work. 2 Corinthians 9:8

The young lions lack and suffer hunger; But those who seek the LORD shall not lack any good thing. Psalm 34:10

Honor the LORD with your possessions, And with the first-fruits of all your increase; So your barns will be filled with plenty, And your vats will overflow with new wine. Proverbs 3:9-10

And my God shall supply all your need according to His riches in glory by Christ Jesus.
Philippians 4:19

If you are willing and obedient, You shall eat the good of the land; Isaiah 1:19

The thief does not come except to steal, and to kill, and to destroy. I have come that they may have life, and that they may have it more abundantly.
John 10:10

Therefore let no one boast in men. For all things are yours : whether Paul or Apollos or Cephas, or the world or life or death, or things present or things to come - all are yours. And you are Christ's, and Christ is God's. 1 Corinthians 3:21-23

And you shall remember the LORD your God, for it is He who gives you power to get wealth, that He may establish His covenant which He swore to your fathers, as it is this day.
Deuteronomy 8:18

Jesus who was rich became poor to pay the price to make me rich. 2 Corinthians 8:9

Therefore, I am rich. I cannot be poor. I always have more than enough in all things. 2 Corinthians 9:8

I am a child of the King. This world and all that exists in the universe belongs to my Father. I am his child. James 1:18

Success is mine. I'm a success. I'm a child of God. If I am his child, I am also a joint-heir with Christ. My life is full of the glory of his inheritance and prosperity. Ephesians 1:18

I know who I am. I am filled with the life of God. I am full of God's power. Christ lives in me. Hallelujah!

In Christ, I am prosperous. I have no lack in material needs. I know that God the Father, who spared not his own son, wants to give me all things.

I believe that when Jesus paid the price for all our curses on the cross, he paid the price for our poverty, and the blessings of Abraham came upon us.

Jesus who owned the whole world was rich, but by becoming poor, he paid the price to make us rich. Therefore, though a young lion may hunger in lack, for me who depends on Jesus, I believe that I have all things in abundance and that I lack nothing.

Because I obey God's Word with a joyful heart, I thank God that he not only fills me with the beautiful fruit of the land, but he also fills me with all that I need according to the glory of his riches.

God always gives me in abundance in all things that I lack nothing in every good work.

I will not use the indescribable abundance he gives me only for myself; I will use them as tools to expand the kingdom of God and to express love to my neighbors.

I will train myself in the principle of sowing and reaping that I may receive a greater blessing with greater faith, that I may be a blessing to others.

My abundance is always filled to overflowing that I always have more than enough to do all the good works God asks me to do.

I will willingly sow and share the prosperity the Lord has committed unto me when he shows me a need and guides me to fill that need.

Confession for a Victorious Family

And said, For this reason a man shall leave his father and mother and be joined to his wife, and the two shall become one flesh? So then, they are no longer two but one flesh. Therefore what God has joined together, let not man separate.

Matthew 19:5-6

But I want you to know that the head of every man is Christ, the head of woman is man, and the head of Christ is God. ⋯ For man is not from woman, but woman from man. Nor was man created for the woman, but woman for the man.

1 Corinthians 11:3, 8-9

1. A Wife's Prayer for her Husband

Wives, likewise, be submissive to your own husbands, that even if some do not obey the word, they, without a word, may be won by the conduct of their wives, when they observe your chaste conduct accompanied by fear.

1 Peter 3:1-2

Wives, submit to your own husbands, as to the Lord. For the husband is head of the wife, as also Christ is head of the church; and He is the Savior of the body. Therefore, just as the church is subject to Christ, so let the wives be to their own husbands in everything.   Ephesians 5:22-24

My husband is the best gift God has given to me. Therefore, I value him and respect him and gladly obey his words.

I am his helper and I always edify and encourage him. As I pray for him, God answers my prayers by helping him to continually grow spiritually, to be a success in his life, and to be a more influential person in the world.

My husband's wisdom is increasing every day.

His ability and capacity is increasing every day.

He is excellent in all things and is recognized as an excellent person even at his work place, favored by his superiors, his colleagues and his subordinates.

He makes the right choices every day and never misses out on a good opportunity, utilizing them to continually make progress and is promoted for it.

2. A Husband's Prayer for his Wife

Husbands, likewise, dwell with them with understanding, giving honor to the wife, as to the weaker vessel, and as being heirs together of the grace of life, that your prayers may not be hindered.
1 Peter 3:7

Husbands, love your wives, just as Christ also loved the church and gave Himself for her ⋯ So husbands ought to love their own wives as their own bodies; he who loves his wife loves himself ⋯ Nevertheless let each one of you in particular so love his own wife as himself, and let the wife see that she respects her husband.
Ephesians 5:25, 28, 33

Her children rise up and call her blessed; Her husband also, and he praises her : "Many daughters have done well, But you excel them all." Charm is deceitful and beauty is passing, But a woman who fears the LORD, she shall be praised. Proverbs 31:28-30

I will consider my wife to be a weaker vessel and value her as an heir together with me in the grace of life.

I love my wife as Christ loved and gave himself for the church.

I value and love my wife as if she was my own body.

My wife is full of wisdom and raises our child with wisdom. My wife continually receives the spirit of wisdom and revelation through the Holy Spirit and grows spiritually everyday as a victor in every area of life.

3. A Parent's Prayer for the Child

And Jesus increased in wisdom and stature, and in favor with God and men. Luke 2:52

And you, fathers, do not provoke your children to wrath, but bring them up in the training and admonition of the Lord. Ephesians 6:4

Fathers, do not provoke your children, lest they become discouraged. Colossians 3:21

Train up a child in the way he should go, And when he is old he will not depart from it.
Proverbs 22:6

The rod and rebuke give wisdom, But a child left to himself brings shame to his mother. Correct your son, and he will give you rest; Yes, he will give delight to your soul. Proverbs 29:15, 17

You shall love the LORD your God with all your heart, with all your soul, and with all your strength. And these words which I command you today shall be in your heart. You shall teach them diligently to your children, and shall talk of them when you sit in your house, when you walk by the way, when you lie down, and when you rise up. You shall bind them as a sign on your hand, and they shall be as frontlets between your eyes. You shall write them on the doorposts of your house and on your gates.   Deuteronomy 6:5-9

My child is the best gift God has given me. Even before God formed him/her in the mother's womb, he created him/her with a plan.

I am a steward to help my child fulfill the plan God has for his/her life.

My child already has all the talent and abilities needed to move forward and succeed up to his/her highest calling. I teach my child the Word and how to apply the Word in his/her life so that he/she may persevere and be diligent in all things, living by faith.

My child is going to be the best in the area of his/her calling. As my child grows in understanding of God's Word, the grace given to him/her will increase more and more and he/she will function excellently in all areas of his/her life. In his/her mouth is wisdom, his/her judgments and choices are excellent, and he/she is favored by his/her superiors and colleagues.

The blessings that go out of my mouth regarding my child become a reality in his/her life.

He/she will grow and increase more and more in wisdom and revelation, and he/she will complete every necessary training to be strongly built up like Joseph, who became an abundantly fruitful branch of the vine, expanding the kingdom of God and manifesting God's glory. Hallelujah!

Confession for Soul-winning

The fruit of the righteous is a tree of life, And he who wins souls is wise. Proverbs 11:30

Those who are wise shall shine Like the brightness of the firmament, And those who turn many to righteousness Like the stars forever and ever.
Daniel 12:3

Who desires all men to be saved and to come to the knowledge of the truth. 1 Timothy 2:4

So they said, "Believe on the Lord Jesus Christ, and you will be saved, you and your household."
Acts 16:31

Father, we come before you in prayer and in faith in the name of Jesus. Jesus came to save the lost. You want all people to be saved and to know your truth. Therefore, Father, we bring (   ) before you today.

Satan, we bind you in the name of Jesus and cast you out in all that you are doing in (   )'s life.

We ask that the Father, the Lord of the harvest, will send a trustworthy worker to (   ) to share the gospel in a special way for him/her to hear the gospel and understand. As your servant serves him/her, he/she will understand the gospel and will become free of the devil's hold on him/her and will serve Jesus to be the Lord of his/her life.

Your word says that you will save those we pray for. We stand upon the Word from this moment on. Father, we thank you for his/her salvation.

We commit this work into the Father's hands.

We see in faith that (   ) is saved, filled with the Holy Spirit, and full of the Word. Amen. Hallelujah!

Pray this prayer everyday and thank the Lord that he/she is saved. Rejoice. Praise God for this victory. Thank Him that Satan is bound. Hallelujah!

[Scripture Reference]
Luke 19:10, 2 Timothy 2:26, Matthew 18:18, Job 22:30, Matthew 9:38,
2 Corinthians 4:4-6, Revelations 20:15, Revelations 21:27, Luke 13:1-5

Confession for Peace

Peace I leave with you, My peace I give to you; not as the world gives do I give to you. Let not your heart be troubled, neither let it be afraid.
John 14:27

Be anxious for nothing, but in everything by prayer and supplication, with thanksgiving, let your requests be made known to God; and the peace of God, which surpasses all understanding, will guard your hearts and minds through Christ Jesus.
Philippians 4:6-7

For the kingdom of God is not eating and drinking, but righteousness and peace and joy in the Holy Spirit.
Romans 14:17

Rejoice always, pray without ceasing, in everything give thanks; for this is the will of God in Christ Jesus for you. Do not quench the Spirit. Do not despise prophecies. Test all things; hold fast what is good. Abstain from every form of evil. Now may the God of peace Himself sanctify you completely; and may your whole spirit, soul, and body be preserved blameless at the coming of our Lord Jesus Christ. He who calls you is faithful, who also will do it.   1 Thessalonians 5:16-24

Lord, I love your Word. You said that to those who love your Word there is no obstacle and there is great peace. That peace has been poured into us through the Holy Spirit and that peace is not like the peace that the world gives. Therefore, I have no need to be worried or afraid.

I am anxious for nothing, but in everything, with prayer and supplication, I make my requests known unto the Father with thanksgiving. I am thankful that when I do so, the peace of God that surpasses all understanding will protect my heart and my mind in Christ Jesus.

Praise the Lord. You said that your kingdom is not eating and drinking, but only righteousness, peace, and joy in the Holy Spirit. Father, continually fill me with your Holy Spirit. I bear more fruits of peace, which is a fruit of the Spirit, in all my relationships.

The peace the Lord has given inside of me is not given by the world, and therefore, the world cannot take it away from me. Because the Lord leads me from peace to peace, as I am strongly rooted, the peace I enjoy from the inside increases more and more. I always have peace in me.

[Scripture Reference]
Psalm 119:165, Psalm 127:2, Isaiah 26:3, Psalm 29:11

Confession for Wisdom and Guidance

However, when He, the Spirit of truth, has come, He will guide you into all truth; for He will not speak on His own authority, but whatever He hears He will speak; and He will tell you things to come. John 16:13

Trust in the LORD with all your heart, And lean not on your own understanding; Proverbs 3:5

The Spirit of truth lives in me and teaches me all things and leads me into all truths. Therefore, I confess that I perfectly know every situation and every circumstance that I face. I have the wisdom of God. John 16:13, James 1:5

I trust the Lord with all my heart and lean not on my own understanding. Proverbs 3:5

In all my ways I acknowledge him, and he will direct my path. Proverbs 3:6

God's Word is a lamp unto my feet and a light unto my path. Psalm 119:105

The Lord will perfect that which concerns me. Psalm 138:8

I let the Word of Christ dwell in me richly in all wisdom. Colossians 3:16

I follow the good shepherd and know his voice. I do not follow a stranger's voice. John 10:4-5

Jesus has become my wisdom, righteousness, sanctification, and redemption. Therefore, I have the wisdom of God. I have become the righteousness of God in Christ Jesus. 1 Corinthians 1:30, 2 Corinthians 5:21

I am full of the knowledge of his will in all divine wisdom and spiritual understanding. Colossians 1:9

I am a new creation in Christ and a masterpiece created in Christ Jesus. Therefore, I have the mind of Christ and the wisdom of God is produced in me. 2 Corinthians 5:17, Ephesians 2:10, 1 Corinthians 2:16

I have put off the old man and have put on the new man, which is renewed in knowledge after the image of him that created me. Colossians 3:10

I have received the spirit of wisdom and revelation, and the eyes of my understanding have been enlightened. I do not conform to this world. I am continually transformed by the renewing of my mind. My mind has been renewed through the Word of God. Ephesians 1:17-18, Romans 12:2

Confession for Victory in Face of Trials

He restores my soul; He leads me in the paths of righteousness For His name's sake.   Psalm 23:3

And not only that, but we also glory in tribulations, knowing that tribulation produces perseverance; and perseverance, character; and character, hope.
Romans 5:3-4

No weapon formed against you shall prosper, And every tongue which rises against you in judgment You shall condemn. This is the heritage of the servants of the LORD, And their righteousness is from Me, Says the LORD.   Isaiah 54:17

For whatever is born of God overcomes the world. And this is the victory that has overcome the world--our faith. 1 John 5:4

No temptation has overtaken you except such as is common to man; but God is faithful, who will not allow you to be tempted beyond what you are able, but with the temptation will also make the way of escape, that you may be able to bear it.
1 Corinthians 10:13

For our light affliction, which is but for a moment, is working for us a far more exceeding and eternal weight of glory, while we do not look at the things which are seen, but at the things which are not seen. For the things which are seen are temporary, but the things which are not seen are eternal.
2 Corinthians 4:17-18

And we know that all things work together for good to those who love God, to those who are the called according to His purpose.   Romans 8:28

The Lord is my shepherd and therefore, I have no lack. I rejoice when I meet tribulation because I believe that this tribulation will work in me patience, and patience, experience; and experience, hope. Romans 5:3-4

No weapon formed against me shall prosper. Isaiah 54:17

I have found my way out of trouble. Everyone that is born of God overcomes the world by faith. I am born of God, and therefore, I overcome the world. 1 John 5:4

I am more than able to overcome all these things through him that loved me. I am more than a conqueror. Romans 8:37

Because the Lord helps me I do not fear what man may do to me. Hebrews 13:6

I stand firm and face the problem. I have more than enough ability to overcome this situation. God is faithful that he would not allow me to face tests that I cannot handle and makes a way out for me in the face of difficulty to be able to handle any situation.

Through the light affliction I experience, I am achieving a spiritual and eternal weight of glory. This trial will only become a stepping stone for me to achieve greater success. I know for sure that all things work together for those who love God and are called according to his purpose.

Confession for Overcoming Fear

Whoever confesses that Jesus is the Son of God, God abides in him, and he in God.   1 John 4:15

I confess that Jesus is the Son of God. Therefore, God lives in me. I live in God.

And we have known and believed the love that God has for us. God is love, and he who abides in love abides in God, and God in him.   1 John 4:16

I know that God loves me. I believe that God loves me. God is love. I live a life of love. I dwell in God and God dwells in me.

There is no fear in love; but perfect love casts out fear, because fear involves torment. But he who fears has not been made perfect in love.

1 John 4:18

God loves me with a perfect love. I am not afraid that God would do something bad to me. I am convinced that God actually loves me. God loves me so much that he cannot leave me the way I am. I trust God completely. I love God because he first loved me.

The LORD is my light and my salvation; Whom shall I fear? The LORD is the strength of my life; Of whom shall I be afraid? Psalm 27:1

The Lord is my light and my salvation. Because he is the strength of my life, I am not afraid of anyone. I have overcome the devil. I do not fear men. I am bold as a lion.

What then shall we say to these things? If God is for us, who can be against us? Romans 8:31

God is on my side. Who could be against me and win? No one. I always win.

He who did not spare His own Son, but delivered Him up for us all, how shall He not with Him also freely give us all things? Romans 8:32

God has already given me the best. God has given me Jesus. I have no lack. I have more than enough to overflowing.

… the one who comes to Me I will by no means cast out. John 6:37

… For He Himself has said, "I will never leave you nor forsake you." Hebrews 13:5

I have come before Jesus. Jesus never leaves

me. God never abandons me. I trust Jesus completely. Jesus is my source. I do not worry whether I can have enough. I always have more than enough.

That Christ may dwell in your hearts through faith; that you, being rooted and grounded in love, may be able to comprehend with all the saints what is the width and length and depth and height -- to know the love of Christ which passes knowledge; that you may be filled with all the fullness of God. Ephesians 3:17-19

I believe Christ lives in me. I have been rooted and grounded in love. I understand the love of Christ, and I have the love of Christ. The Anointed One lives in me.

Therefore submit to God. Resist the devil and he will flee from you. James 4:7

No weapon formed against you shall prosper, And every tongue which rises against you in judgment You shall condemn. This is the heritage of the servants of the LORD, And their righteousness is from Me," Says the LORD.

Isaiah 54:17

I am not afraid of the devil. When I resist the devil, he cannot help but flee. Any of his strategies or tactics are useless on me.

You are of God, little children, and have overcome them, because He who is in you is greater than he who is in the world. 1 John 4:4

The wisdom of man and the wisdom of the world says that "Life is full of ups and downs." But even though I live in the world, I am not of the world, so I keep moving upwards and forwards. There is no retreat or regression in my life.

I only think progress and success. Failure does

not exist in my life. I am more than a conqueror through Christ who makes me overcome. Romans 8:37 Nothing can shake me or change my mind. No situation or person can hinder my success, because success is inside of me. Hallelujah!

Prayer for Beginning the Day

Father, in the name of the Lord Jesus, I understand from the Word of God that you'll take charge of my circumstances if I let you.

You are the Lord of my life, and I pray that you order my steps today in the course that you've already planned for me.

I want to meet only the people that you plan for me to meet today, and hear the things that you plan for me to hear, and say the things you plan for me to say.

I function as a child of God today in the anointing of the Holy Ghost.

I walk in your light, in the name of the Lord Jesus.

There's nobody coming into my world as an

accident today.

The Spirit of dominion is at work in me today, in the name of the Lord Jesus.

I refuse to fear, for though I walk through the valley of the shadow of death, I fear no evil, for you are with me; Your rod and your staff comfort me.

I refuse to be defeated today, for I'm a victor in Christ Jesus. I'm more than a conqueror, in the name of the Lord Jesus.

Thank you, Lord, for your presence is with me today. I thank you for the Spirit of excellence is at work in me.

I do not act foolishly or utter a foolish word. The wisdom of God is found in my mouth, and I give counsel by the Spirit today.

I deal with people by the Spirit today. I see with the eyes of God today, in the name of the Lord Jesus Christ.

Oh, Lord, I thank you, because good things are coming my way today. I receive them in the name of the Lord Jesus. And I'm a giver today; I'm a blesser today, in the name of the Lord Jesus. Whoever meets me today is blessed. Being in Christ, I am the source of blessing.

My body is yielded to you. Every fiber of my being and every bone of my body is for the Holy Ghost.

I'm your living tabernacle today. Talk through me; move through me; walk in me; talk in me, in the name of the Lord Jesus. I will obey your Word.

Divine health is in me. I refuse to let my body be subject to sickness, disease and infirmity. Every fiber of my being is inundated by the life of God. I'm walking in divine health, in the name of Jesus. Glory to God!

Lord, I thank you for the Spirit of understanding and the Spirit of knowledge are functioning in me. I study the Word of God today and I understand it. As I see and hear the Word, I can understand the Word, and that Word will work in me, and my mouth will keep on speaking it. I will speak boldly concerning the things of God and the revelations of God that I receive, in the name of the Lord Jesus.

The nations of the world are waiting for me, and I'm coming in the name of the Lord. I've been commissioned and sent of God. I've got a message from him to the world, and they will hear it, in the name of Jesus. Watch out world, I'm coming!

• For The Family

I thank you Father for my precious children. Your anointing is upon them. They can't but do the will of God. They can't but work the works of God. They can't but live in the Word of God, in the name of Jesus.

No devil hatched out of hell can touch them.

I thank you Father, for wisdom is in the mouth

of my wife(husband) and in her/his heart. She/he functions in the things of God today, in the name of the Lord Jesus.

• For the Staff

I pray for every one of my staff in the name of Jesus. They cannot but do the will of God and think the thoughts of God. In their going out and in their coming in, not one of them is subject to the devil. The Word of God is in their hearts and in their mouths in the name of the Lord Jesus!

I begin the day with the Holy Spirit, full of strength. I can do all things in Christ, according to his anointing. I am victorious in every situation I meet today. I am moving forward and winning today. I praise the King of glory. Hallelujah!

• For my Cell Members

Lord, thank you for our beloved cell family you have sent to me. I bless them and pray for them in Jesus name. Today they will walk with Christ in the Lord. The word alive in them will work in them, and as the Holy Spirit guides them and reveals things to them, they will react sensitively and move forward from glory to glory and from strength to strength. They will walk in your best path of blessing which you've prepared for them. They will not only receive the best favor by meeting people you have prepared, but will also become a blessing to everyone they meet. An opportunity to win souls is opening for them. They are growing, being promoted, and moving forward. Everywhere they go, God's anointing is with them, and they will finish today with a victorious testimony in Jesus name.

Metamorphosis

Part Ⅲ

Appendix

And these words which I command you today
shall be in your heart.
You shall teach them diligently to your children,
and shall talk of them when you sit in your house,
when you walk by the way,
when you lie down, and when you rise up.
You shall bind them as a sign on your hand,
and they shall be as frontlets between your eyes.
You shall write them on the doorposts of your house
and on your gates.
Deuteronomy 6:6-9

Confessions from Foundation of Faith

1. Freedom

Then Jesus said to those Jews who believed Him, If you abide in My word, you are My disciples indeed. And you shall know the truth, and the truth shall make you free. John 8:31-32

Sanctify them by Your truth. Your word is truth.
John 17:17

I desire to receive the Word of God by his grace and not by my own righteousness. I refuse legalistic mindsets and judging attitudes in the name of Jesus.

I do not approach the Word of God by moral standards. I see and understand the Bible through the eyes of the gospel.

I do not interpret the Bible based on my experience, worldly theories or knowledge. I refuse to put these things above the authority of the Word of God.

I believe that the truth sets me free as I speak, think, and act according to the Word of God.

To Him who loved us and washed us from our sins in His own blood, and has made us kings and priests to His God and Father, to Him be glory and dominion forever and ever. Amen.

Revelation 1:5-6

2. Confession of Faith

You are the Christ, the Son of the living God.
Matthew 16:16

But as many as received Him, to them He gave the right to become children of God, to those who believe in His name :　　　　　　John 1:12

Even when we were dead in trespasses, made us alive together with Christ (by grace you have been saved), and raised us up together, and made us sit together in the heavenly places in Christ Jesus,　　　　　　Ephesians 2:5-6

　By receiving Christ, I was born again as a new creation. I have been seated in the place of authority with Christ Jesus. I hereby declare that I see all circumstances through the Word, and I reign over them by proclaiming in faith.

3. Who is a Christian?

• One who functions as a new creation

Therefore, if anyone is in Christ, he is a new creation; old things have passed away; behold, all things have become new.   2 Corinthians 5:17

• One who lives by the life of God

And this is the testimony : that God has given us eternal life, and this life is in His Son. He who has the Son has life; he who does not have the Son of God does not have life.   1 John 5:11-12

• One who has overcome the world and who reigns in the world

You are of God, little children, and have overcome them, because He who is in you is greater than he who is in the world.   1 John 4:4

- **One who lives by faith**

Therefore, if anyone is in Christ, he is a new creation; old things have passed away; behold, all things have become new.   2 Corinthians 5:17

So the Lord said, "If you have faith as a mustard seed, you can say to this mulberry tree, 'Be pulled up by the roots and be planted in the sea,' and it would obey you.   Luke 17:6

- **One who has been made righteous by the righteousness of God**

Being justified freely by His grace through the redemption that is in Christ Jesus,   Romans 3:24

Who was delivered up because of our offenses, and was raised because of our justification.
Romans 4:25

For if by the one man's offense death reigned through the one, much more those who receive abundance of grace and of the gift of righteousness will reign in life through the One, Jesus Christ.

Romans 5:17

As a Christian, I have eternal life. This ZOE life is a life-giving spirit. Therefore, no sickness can stay in my body. When I meet circumstances that I do not like, I change the situation by proclaiming in faith.

As a Christian, I am superior to Satan.

I have faith.

I am righteous. Righteousness is my nature.

I can always stand in the presence of God without any guilt or inferiority regardless of my actions.

I have the grace to do all things excellently.

As an actual child of God, I reign over all circumstances as Jesus did on the earth. I am the righteousness of God.

I am the trophy of God's goodness.

4. Prayer

And whatever you ask in My name, that I will do, that the Father may be glorified in the Son. If you ask anything in My name, I will do it.

John 14:13-14

If you abide in Me, and My words abide in you, you will ask what you desire, and it shall be done for you.   John 15:7

You did not choose Me, but I chose you and appointed you that you should go and bear fruit, and that your fruit should remain, that whatever you ask the Father in My name He may give you.

John 15:16

God has chosen me and ordained me so that he could answer my prayer.

I ask for what I need today in prayer in the name of Jesus according to the word of God. I believe I have already received what I have asked for. My prayers are always answered because God is faithful.

5. Being Led by the Holy Spirit

But the Helper, the Holy Spirit, whom the Father will send in My name, He will teach you all things, and bring to your remembrance all things that I said to you. John 14:26

My sheep hear My voice, and I know them, and they follow Me. John 10:27

For as many as are led by the Spirit of God, these are sons of God. Romans 8:14

    I hear the voice of the Lord because I am his sheep. As the Lord abides in me, he guides me in various ways in everything that I trust him with. I enjoy a more abundant Christian life by committing more areas of my life to be led by him.

6. Foundational Doctrine Ⅰ

All Scripture is given by inspiration of God, and is profitable for doctrine, for reproof, for correction, for instruction in righteousness,   2 Timothy 3:16

You are of God, little children, and have overcome them, because He who is in you is greater than he who is in the world.   1 John 4:4

Therefore submit to God. Resist the devil and he will flee from you.   James 4:7

   I believe in the sovereignty of God, who reigns over the universe, and in the redemption of Jesus Christ. I rely on the Holy Spirit who is still alive and working and helping me today.
   I believe all Scripture is written by the inspiration of God and is the unchanging truth. I proclaim that I will think, speak and live according to the word of truth. I know that Satan is a

disarmed enemy. I confront his deceptions with the word of God and always triumph over him. I declare that all theft and destroying works of the enemy are illegal.

7. Fundamental Doctrine Ⅱ

But you shall receive power when the Holy Spirit has come upon you; and you shall be witnesses to Me in Jerusalem, and in all Judea and Samaria, and to the end of the earth. Acts 1:8

 I believe that there is no coincidence for a Christian. Therefore, I give my all during worship and fulfill the will of God in all encounters and incidents, living every moment to the best of my ability.
 I do not get caught up in the praise or criticism of men, for the Lord knows everything about me. Instead, I am conscious of God who reigns over the universe and only desire his approval.
 I am a spirit, I have a soul, and I live in a body. I am a weapon of righteousness. My soul submits to my spirit and my flesh submits to my renewed soul as I confess the Word.
 As a Christian, I no longer live for myself, but I

have set my life's direction for the glory of God, the benefits of others, and the spread of the gospel, living as a wise, victorious, and happy pilgrim.

8. God's Divine Character

The thief does not come except to steal, and to kill, and to destroy. I have come that they may have life, and that they may have it more abundantly. John 10:10

God is good and the devil is bad. I believe in his goodness, his might, and his righteousness. He faithfully works according to his promise whenever I get a hold of his word.

I joyfully obey the Word of God today because I believe that God is love and that he always gives me freedom.

God is the same yesterday, today and forever and he does not look at men's appearance. He works for me in the same way as he did for the righteous men of both the Old and New Testament when I get hold of the Word he has given to them.

9. Nine Gifts of the Holy Spirit

There are diversities of gifts, but the same Spirit. There are differences of ministries, but the same Lord. And there are diversities of activities, but it is the same God who works all in all. But the manifestation of the Spirit is given to each one for the profit of all :   1 Corinthians 12:4-7

But earnestly desire the best gifts. And yet I show you a more excellent way.   1 Corinthians 12:31

I eagerly desire the gifts of the Holy Spirit today. I desire the word of knowledge, the word of wisdom, discerning of spirits, the gifts of healing, faith, the working of miracles, diverse kinds of tongues, prophecy, the interpretation of tongues to be manifested in my life, in my cell, and in my church in such abundance that we may become powerful Christians and a powerful church.

10. Faith

So then faith comes by hearing, and hearing by the word of God. Romans 10:17

But without faith it is impossible to please Him, for he who comes to God must believe that He is, and that He is a rewarder of those who diligently seek Him. Hebrews 11:6

For we walk by faith, not by sight.
2 Corinthians 5:7

Now the just shall live by faith; But if anyone draws back, My soul has no pleasure in him.
Hebrews 10:38

   I seek and enjoy the blessings of God's promises by faith today. Faith comes by hearing the Word of God and the Word works when I confess it. I live by faith, not by sight. My faith is increasing every day.

11. Spiritual Growth

For the equipping of the saints for the work of ministry, for the edifying of the body of Christ,
Ephesians 4:12

But we all, with unveiled face, beholding as in a mirror the glory of the Lord, are being transformed into the same image from glory to glory, just as by the Spirit of the Lord.   2 Corinthians 3:18

Today, I humbly receive the Word of God regarding new creation realities with a teachable spirit, applying the Word of righteousness to my life with patience, and growing spiritually every day. I am a fruitful branch of the vine who bears fruit in season by continually growing until I come to the measure of the stature of the fullness of Christ, looking into the perfect law that gives me freedom, and being changed from glory to glory by the Holy Spirit.

12. The Hope of His Calling

As You sent Me into the world, I also have sent them into the world. John 17:18

Therefore if anyone cleanses himself from the latter, he will be a vessel for honor, sanctified and useful for the Master, prepared for every good work. 2 Timothy 2:21

Moreover it is required in stewards that one be found faithful. 1 Corinthians 4:2

I live in the world, but I am not of the world. I belong to the kingdom of heaven and I shine forth the light of Jesus in the world. I believe the Holy Spirit in me is guiding me to my highest calling as I faithfully complete the small tasks I am entrusted with today. I am a pilgrim who voluntarily serves Jesus as Lord, obeying his voice every day.

Confessions from Psalms

Psalm 1:1-3

1 Blessed is the man Who walks not in the counsel of the ungodly, Nor stands in the path of sinners, Nor sits in the seat of the scornful;
2 But his delight is in the law of the LORD, And in His law he meditates day and night.
3 He shall be like a tree Planted by the rivers of water, That brings forth its fruit in its season, Whose leaf also shall not wither; And whatever he does shall prosper.

Psalm 23

1 The LORD is my shepherd; I shall not want.
2 He makes me to lie down in green pastures; He leads me beside the still waters.

3 He restores my soul; He leads me in the paths of righteous-ness For His name's sake.

4 Yea, though I walk through the valley of the shadow of death, I will fear no evil; For You are with me; Your rod and Your staff, they comfort me.

5 You prepare a table before me in the presence of my enemies; You anoint my head with oil; My cup runs over.

6 Surely goodness and mercy shall follow me All the days of my life; And I will dwell in the house of the LORD Forever.

Psalm 91

1 He who dwells in the secret place of the Most High Shall abide under the shadow of the Almighty.

2 I will say of the LORD, "He is my refuge and my fortress; My God, in Him I will trust."

3 Surely He shall deliver you from the snare of the fowler And from the perilous pestilence.

4 He shall cover you with His feathers, And under

His wings you shall take refuge; His truth shall be your shield and buckler.

5 You shall not be afraid of the terror by night, Nor of the arrow that flies by day,

6 Nor of the pestilence that walks in darkness, Nor of the destruction that lays waste at noonday.

7 A thousand may fall at your side, And ten thousand at your right hand; But it shall not come near you.

8 Only with your eyes shall you look, And see the reward of the wicked.

9 Because you have made the LORD, who is my refuge, Even the Most High, your dwelling place,

10 No evil shall befall you, Nor shall any plague come near your dwelling;

11 For He shall give His angels charge over you, To keep you in all your ways.

12 In their hands they shall bear you up, Lest you dash your foot against a stone.

13 You shall tread upon the lion and the cobra, The young lion and the serpent you shall trample underfoot.

¹⁴ Because he has set his love upon Me, therefore I will deliver him; I will set him on high, because he has known My name.

¹⁵ He shall call upon Me, and I will answer him; I will be with him in trouble; I will deliver him and honor him.

¹⁶ With long life I will satisfy him, And show him My salvation.

Psalm 103:1-5

¹ Bless the LORD, O my soul; And all that is within me, bless His holy name!

² Bless the LORD, O my soul, And forget not all His benefits :

³ Who forgives all your iniquities, Who heals all your diseases,

⁴ Who redeems your life from destruction, Who crowns you with lovingkindness and tender mercies,

⁵ Who satisfies your mouth with good things, So that your youth is renewed like the eagle's.

Psalm 127

1 A Song of Ascents. Of Solomon. Unless the LORD builds the house, They labor in vain who build it; Unless the LORD guards the city, The watchman stays awake in vain.

2 It is vain for you to rise up early, To sit up late, To eat the bread of sorrows; For so He gives His beloved sleep.

3 Behold, children are a heritage from the LORD, The fruit of the womb is a reward.

4 Like arrows in the hand of a warrior, So are the children of one's youth.

5 Happy is the man who has his quiver full of them; They shall not be ashamed, But shall speak with their enemies in the gate.

Psalm 128

1 A Song of Ascents. Blessed is every one who fears the LORD, Who walks in His ways.

2 When you eat the labor of your hands, You shall be happy, and it shall be well with you.

3 Your wife shall be like a fruitful vine In the very heart of your house, Your children like olive plants All around your table.

4 Behold, thus shall the man be blessed Who fears the LORD.

5 The LORD bless you out of Zion, And may you see the good of Jerusalem All the days of your life.

6 Yes, may you see your children's children. Peace be upon Israel!

Psalm 133

1 Behold, how good and how pleasant it is For brethren to dwell together in unity!

2 It is like the precious oil upon the head, Running down on the beard, The beard of Aaron, Running down on the edge of his garments.

3 It is like the dew of Hermon, Descending upon the mountains of Zion; For there the LORD commanded the blessing--Life forevermore.

Romans 8

¹ There is therefore now no condemnation to those who are in Christ Jesus, who do not walk according to the flesh, but according to the Spirit.

² For the law of the Spirit of life in Christ Jesus has made me free from the law of sin and death.

³ For what the law could not do in that it was weak through the flesh, God did by sending His own Son in the likeness of sinful flesh, on account of sin : He condemned sin in the flesh,

⁴ that the righteous requirement of the law might be fulfilled in us who do not walk according to the flesh but according to the Spirit.

⁵ For those who live according to the flesh set their minds on the things of the flesh, but those who live according to the Spirit, the things of the Spirit.

6 For to be carnally minded is death, but to be spiritually minded is life and peace.

7 Because the carnal mind is enmity against God; for it is not subject to the law of God, nor indeed can be.

8 So then, those who are in the flesh cannot please God.

9 But you are not in the flesh but in the Spirit, if indeed the Spirit of God dwells in you. Now if anyone does not have the Spirit of Christ, he is not His.

10 And if Christ is in you, the body is dead because of sin, but the Spirit is life because of righteousness.

11 But if the Spirit of Him who raised Jesus from the dead dwells in you, He who raised Christ from the dead will also give life to your mortal bodies through His Spirit who dwells in you.

12 Therefore, brethren, we are debtors--not to the flesh, to live according to the flesh.

13 For if you live according to the flesh you will

die; but if by the Spirit you put to death the deeds of the body, you will live.

14 For as many as are led by the Spirit of God, these are sons of God.

15 For you did not receive the spirit of bondage again to fear, but you received the Spirit of adoption by whom we cry out, "Abba, Father."

16 The Spirit Himself bears witness with our spirit that we are children of God,

17 and if children, then heirs--heirs of God and joint heirs with Christ, if indeed we suffer with Him, that we may also be glorified together.

18 For I consider that the sufferings of this present time are not worthy to be compared with the glory which shall be revealed in us.

19 For the earnest expectation of the creation eagerly waits for the revealing of the sons of God.

20 For the creation was subjected to futility, not willingly, but because of Him who subjected it in hope;

²¹ because the creation itself also will be delivered from the bondage of corruption into the glorious liberty of the children of God.

²² For we know that the whole creation groans and labors with birth pangs together until now.

²³ Not only that, but we also who have the firstfruits of the Spirit, even we ourselves groan within ourselves, eagerly waiting for the adoption, the redemption of our body.

²⁴ For we were saved in this hope, but hope that is seen is not hope; for why does one still hope for what he sees?

²⁵ But if we hope for what we do not see, we eagerly wait for it with perseverance.

²⁶ Likewise the Spirit also helps in our weaknesses. For we do not know what we should pray for as we ought, but the Spirit Himself makes intercession for us with groanings which cannot be uttered.

²⁷ Now He who searches the hearts knows what the mind of the Spirit is, because He makes

intercession for the saints according to the will of God.

²⁸ And we know that all things work together for good to those who love God, to those who are the called according to His purpose.

²⁹ For whom He foreknew, He also predestined to be conformed to the image of His Son, that He might be the firstborn among many brethren.

³⁰ Moreover whom He predestined, these He also called; whom He called, these He also justified; and whom He justified, these He also glorified.

³¹ What then shall we say to these things? If God is for us, who can be against us?

³² He who did not spare His own Son, but delivered Him up for us all, how shall He not with Him also freely give us all things?

³³ Who shall bring a charge against God's elect? It is God who justifies.

³⁴ Who is he who condemns? It is Christ who died, and furthermore is also risen, who is even

at the right hand of God, who also makes intercession for us.

35 Who shall separate us from the love of Christ? Shall tribulation, or distress, or persecution, or famine, or nakedness, or peril, or sword?

36 As it is written : "For Your sake we are killed all day long; We are accounted as sheep for the slaughter."

37 Yet in all these things we are more than conquerors through Him who loved us.

38 For I am persuaded that neither death nor life, nor angels nor principalities nor powers, nor things present nor things to come,

39 nor height nor depth, nor any other created thing, shall be able to separate us from the love of God which is in Christ Jesus our Lord.

Isaiah 60

¹ Arise, shine; For your light has come! And the glory of the LORD is risen upon you.

² For behold, the darkness shall cover the earth, And deep darkness the people; But the LORD will arise over you, And His glory will be seen upon you.

³ The Gentiles shall come to your light, And kings to the brightness of your rising.

⁴ Lift up your eyes all around, and see : They all gather together, they come to you; Your sons shall come from afar, And your daughters shall be nursed at your side.

⁵ Then you shall see and become radiant, And your heart shall swell with joy; Because the abundance of the sea shall be turned to you, The wealth of the Gentiles shall come to you.

⁶ The multitude of camels shall cover your land, The dromedaries of Midian and Ephah; All those from Sheba shall come; They shall bring gold and incense, And they shall proclaim the praises of the LORD.

⁷ All the flocks of Kedar shall be gathered together to you, The rams of Nebaioth shall minister to you; They shall ascend with acceptance on My altar, And I will glorify the house of My glory.

⁸ Who are these who fly like a cloud, And like doves to their roosts?

⁹ Surely the coastlands shall wait for Me; And the ships of Tarshish will come first, To bring your sons from afar, Their silver and their gold with them, To the name of the LORD your God, And to the Holy One of Israel, Because He has glorified you.

¹⁰ The sons of foreigners shall build up your walls, And their kings shall minister to you; For in My wrath I struck you, But in My favor I have had mercy on you.

11 Therefore your gates shall be open continually; They shall not be shut day or night, That men may bring to you the wealth of the Gentiles, And their kings in procession.

12 For the nation and kingdom which will not serve you shall perish, And those nations shall be utterly ruined.

13 The glory of Lebanon shall come to you, The cypress, the pine, and the box tree together, To beautify the place of My sanctuary; And I will make the place of My feet glorious.

14 Also the sons of those who afflicted you Shall come bowing to you, And all those who despised you shall fall prostrate at the soles of your feet; And they shall call you The City of the LORD, Zion of the Holy One of Israel.

15 Whereas you have been forsaken and hated, So that no one went through you, I will make you an eternal excellence, A joy of many generations.

16 You shall drink the milk of the Gentiles, And milk the breast of kings; You shall know that I, the

LORD, am your Savior And your Redeemer, the Mighty One of Jacob.

17 Instead of bronze I will bring gold, Instead of iron I will bring silver, Instead of wood, bronze, And instead of stones, iron. I will also make your officers peace, And your magistrates righteousness.

18 Violence shall no longer be heard in your land, Neither wasting nor destruction within your borders; But you shall call your walls Salvation, And your gates Praise.

19 The sun shall no longer be your light by day, Nor for brightness shall the moon give light to you; But the LORD will be to you an everlasting light, And your God your glory.

20 Your sun shall no longer go down, Nor shall your moon withdraw itself; For the LORD will be your everlasting light, And the days of your mourning shall be ended.

21 Also your people shall all be righteous; They shall inherit the land forever, The branch of My

planting, The work of My hands, That I may be glorified.

22 A little one shall become a thousand, And a small one a strong nation. I, the LORD, will hasten it in its time.

Metamorphosis

Part IV

Understanding the Principles of Confession

My son, pay attention to what I say; listen closely to my words. Do not let them out of your sight, keep them within your heart; for they are life to those who find them and health to a man's whole body. Proverbs 4:20-22(NIV)

Just as a sick person would feel better after taking the prescription a doctor has given them, a Christian who takes the Word of God according to God's Word is bound to taste the effects of the Word. Proverbs 4:20-22 tells us the way in which we should take a hold of God's Word. This scripture is a Word in which a parent gives to a child, showing how Christians should read, study, confess, and proclaim God's Word.

Because we live in a negative world, modern day people are exposed to so much news, advertisements, and information on the internet 24 hours a day through the smartphones they carry around with them all the time. Just as voice fishing and hackers are always eyeing on the money in your bank account, there is overflowing information at the touch of our fingers eyeing for our hearts. The moment we read these kinds of information we are easily infected by viruses of anxiety and worry, fear and lack, criticism and negative thoughts. Each person's developmental background and experiences can also be left as bitter roots deep in the heart if they are not resolved with forgiveness and reconciliation. Even people who have left the world and live in a monastery cannot help but influence one another in the community they live in. Therefore, as we live in this world, we need to learn how to "live by every word that comes out of the mouth of God" in our daily lives. If we do not learn to do this then we would just live according to the manners of this world as a spiritual infant, unable to change the world.

That's why the Lord said that man does not live by bread alone, but that we are beings that live by "every word that comes out of the mouth of God" - rhema. Even in "the parable of the sower," the Lord said that each person sows a "seed" of the Word in the "field" of their spirits and harvest fruit. Man is a spiritual being made to speak whatever fills his heart. Each person is programmed like a computer, allowing which things to enter into his heart and intentionally piling good things inside of them, which become good resources to think good thoughts, to speak good words, and to make good choices to live a good life. This means they live and function according to the software they have downloaded, according to the way they were programmed.

You brood of vipers, how can you who are evil say anything good / For out of the overflow of the heart the mouth speaks. The good man brings good things out of the good stored up in him, and the evil man brings evil things out of the evil stored up in him.   Matthew 12:34-35(NIV)

Just as we use the best anti-virus software program to block out virus infection, we must accept God's pure word that hasn't been infected by "the traditions of men" to bear good fruit.

Thus have ye made the commandment of God of none effect by your tradition.   Matthew 15:6(KJV)

Thus you nullify the word of God for the sake of your tradition.   Matthew 15:6(NIV)

Not only that, we should always watch out to never blindly accept any outside information that comes through the five senses and train ourselves to filter them to accept only what is good.

Keep your heart with all diligence, For out of it spring the issues of life.   Proverbs 4:23

Our spirit is the most important place we must

guard. "To keep with all diligence" means an attitude of being completely on guard as a soldier who is standing on guard to prevent the enemy from penetrating. Just as banks or important government information departments protect themselves from hackers and computer viruses through developing programs and strengthening their security through hardware and physical means, one must guard one's heart. Proverbs 4:23 says that the heart of man is where "the issues of life" come, meaning that everything in life comes from the heart. Not only should we have thorough defense, there also needs to be proactive and intentional input of God's Word in one's spirit. One simple principle of a computer's information processing is "Garbage in, garbage out." This means that good data needs to be put in in order to produce trustworthy results. A person's spirit, soul, and body is like a giant computer in that whatever is put in comes out in the background. In other words, the life I live today is a product of the choices I have made based on all the things that have come into my heart.

Deuteronomy chapter 6 accurately teaches us how to program a person according to the Word of God. This method has been proved to be effective in the Jewish family education for over 3000 years. It was the parents' responsibility to thoroughly train a child to make it a habit and for the Word of God to become his personal mindset.

> Repeat them again and again to your children. Talk about them when you are at home and when you are on the road, when you are going to bed and when you are getting up. Tie them to your hands and wear them on your forehead as reminders. Write them on the doorposts of your house and on your gates. Deuteronomy 6:7-9(NLT)

Even now we see that the Jews exercise a

heavy influence on the financial and political systems of America which is the center of the world economy, as well as the humanities and the sciences. This shows that their method was effective. Even brain science, psychology, and educational studies on how to raise creative human resources that would lead in the arts, design, and technological innovations show that this Jewish way of education based on Scripture has proven to be very effective. Even more so, the desire for excellent leaders that are equipped with character and ability shows the importance of biblical education. Even the Apostle Paul teaches his beloved disciple Timothy what he needs to give himself wholly to. This is the New Testament model we must follow after.

Meditate upon these things; give thyself wholly to them; that thy profiting may appear to all.
1 Timothy 4:15(KJV)

Practice these things, immerse yourself in them, so that all may see your progress.

> 1 Timothy 4:15(ESV)

Give your complete attention to these matters. Throw yourself into your tasks so that everyone will see your progress.   1 Timothy 4:15(NLT)

What Paul is saying to give yourself wholly to is mentioned in verse 13, which is reading, exhortation, and doctrine. This is not just meditation and memorizing on your own, but being able to teach and exhort others so that they may also be able to enjoy the benefits of the gospel you are enjoying. What comes out of your mouth should be an overflow of the Word of God you have been feeding your spirit. This naturally becomes a part of one's mindset, a habit of thought, and a standard for making good choices, making God's Word the only light to one's path, and lamp unto one's feet.

Man was made not only to have himself hear and remember the words his mouth speaks, but was made to have that word carved into his spirit if he repeats it enough. As a result, the Word of God overflowing in my spirit renews the thoughts of my mind and finally even the words that come out of my mouth can only be perfect words.

It is the Spirit who gives life; the flesh profits nothing. The words that I speak to you are spirit, and they are life. John 6:63

A man will be satisifed with good by the fruit of his mouth, And the recompense of a man's hands will be rendered to him. Proverbs 12:14

For we all stumble in many things. If anyone does not stumble in word, he is a perfect man, able also to bridle the whole body. James 3:2

The best habit that a victorious reigning-in-life

Christian should have is to personally study the Word, pray in the spirit, plant the Word in his heart by confessing the Word, and continually speaking it to activate the anointing inside. The Apostle Paul said in his letter to Philemon that the key was to acknowledge, confess, and proclaim the good things which was in him in Christ Jesus.

That the communication of thy faith may become effectual by the acknowledging of every good thing which is in you in Christ.　　Philemon 1:6(KJV)

When the thoughts of Christ become my thoughts, words, habits, and actions, the Lord describes this state as the relationship between the vine and the branch.

If you abide in Me, and My words abide in you, you will ask what you desire, and it shall be done for you.　　　　　　　　　　　　　　　　John 15:7

This confession book has taken the most important keys of the gospel to be confessed daily, and many saints of the church are experiencing what the Word speaks about. This is the best spiritual habit that the bible guarantees to take every Christian from glory to glory, to not only show forth the glory of Christ that is in them, but to help guide each one of us to fulfill one's highest calling.

2014 January

Rev. **Jinho Kim**

Representative of New Creation Ministry
Principal of Jesus Missions Academy